Crossword Puzzles for Kids Ages 6 - 8
90 Crossword Easy Puzzle Book

This book includes free bonus that are available here:
www.funspace.club
Follow us: facebook.com/funspaceclub

Introduction

This crosswords puzzle book contain English words for kids 6 - 8 years olds. Crosswords is a very easy and simple game. It's fun & educate kids. You just have to have a good stock of words. Look at empty boxes. By default, the game takes you through the clues in order starting with clue 1. After you fill in a clue you are taken to the next one. You have to fill up those across (horizontal) empty boxes and down (vertical) empty boxes with the right words and phrases by using clue to get idea.

See more great books for kids at

www.funspace.club

Follow us : facebook.com/funspaceclub

Send email to get answer & solution here : funspaceclub18@gmail.com

Body

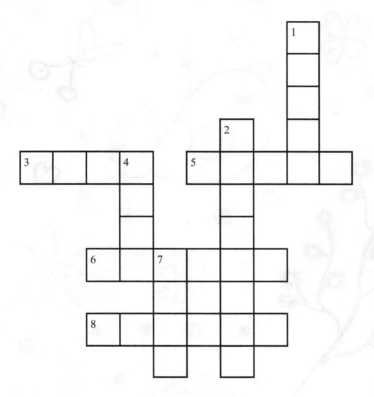

Across

3. It is the outer covering of your body.

5. It is the bony structure of head that encloses the brain and supports the jaws.

6. People have five _____: sight, hearing, smell, taste and touch.

8. They take care of you when your body is sick.

Down

1. It looks like a black circle in the middle of an eye.

2. It is a set of bones in a body.

4. We use this to breathe and also gives us a sense of smell.

7. It is between your head and shoulder.

Shape

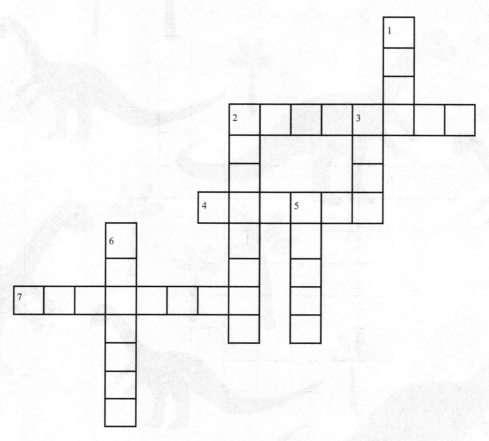

Across

2. It is a curved shape that is wider in the middle than at its ends, like the shape of the moon during its first and last quarters.

4. It is round shape.

7. It has three straight sides and three vertices.

Down

1. A box-shaped solid object that has six identical square faces.

2. It is a solid with circular base like the shape of a pillar, a rubber tube and the trunk of a tree.

3. A shape whose base is a circle and whose sides taper up to a point like a container that holds ice cream.

5. It is a wavy line.

6. It is a quadrilateral, a 2 dimensional flat figure that has four closed, straight sides and also categorized as rhombus.

Nutrients

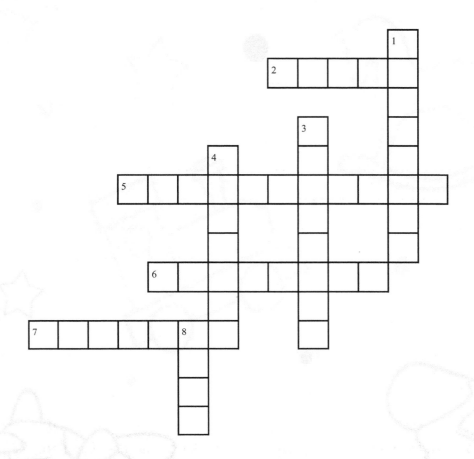

Across

2. Found in whole grains, fruits and vegetables and it keeps our digestive system healthy.

5. It is a type of fat found in your blood. The body needs some of it, but too much can be a problem.

6. Build tissues and repairs body cells.

7. A unit of heat used to measure the energy value of food.

Down

1. It is a natural sugar that is present in fruits, fruit juices, certain vegetables, and honey.

3. _____ are a group of substances that are needed for normal cell function, growth, and development.

4. A simple sugar that our body uses for quick energy.

8. It is a mineral and it carries oxygen in the hemoglobin of red blood cells throughout the body.

School

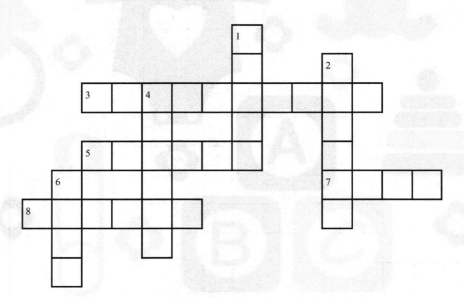

Across

3. It is a book that contains the meaning of different words.

5. A mark indicating the quality of a student's work.

7. An _____ is a test.

8. It is a structured period of time where learning is intended to occur.

Down

1. Physical object that are excellent sources for information.

2. It rubs off pencil marks.

4. It is a pencil or stick of colored chalk or wax, used for drawing.

6. A piece of furniture at which one can read and write.

School

Across

3. Acquired knowledge of or skill in by study, experience, or being taught.

6. Device that makes pencil sharp.

Down

1. An instrument for writing or drawing.

2. It is a material that you write on.

3. A place set apart to contain books, periodicals, and other material for reading.

4. Learning something so that you will remember it exactly.

5. A small book with blank or ruled pages for writing notes in.

Body

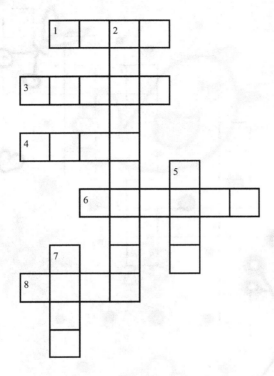

Across

1. It is a colored part of the eye around the pupil.

3. We use it to eat and talk.

4. Your _____ are below your waist and above your legs.

6. It is a bean-shaped organs that takes waste from the blood and produce urine.

8. These let you open and close your mouth and take bites.

Down

2. These are part of the digestive system that help digest foods, absorb it into the body and excrete waste.

5. It is where the leg bends.

7. It is a hard scale that grows at the end of your finger.

School

Across

3. A bag with shoulder straps that allow it to be carried on one's back.

4. A test of knowledge, especially a brief, informal test given to students.

5. It is a dark-coloured board that you can write on with chalk and it is also called blackboard.

6. A system of letters of a language written or spoken in their proper order from A-Z.

Down

1. A small electronic device that is used for doing calculations.

2. A piece of furniture with shelves to hold books.

5. It is a diagram , picture , or graph which is intended to make information easier.

7. A mixture of flour and water, often with starch or the like, used for causing paper or other material to adhere to something.

Adjectives

Across

2. Empty is the opposite of it.
4. When we are afraid.
6. It is not clean.

Down

1. Extremely good.
2. The opposite of thin.
3. When people act nicely to each other.
5. It occurs before it was expected to happen.

Science

Across

4. It is a temperature scale and also known as the centigrade scale.

6. It is a thin layer of gases that hover above our planet's surface.

7. It is a proposed explanation for a phenomenon.

8. Rainfall made sufficiently acidic by atmospheric pollution that it causes environmental harm, typically to forests and lakes.

Down

1. It is a visible mass of small water droplets or ice particles which are suspended in the sky.

2. It is a storm of rapidly spinning air that is very dangerous.

3. It is the process of a substance in a liquid state changing to a gaseous state due to an increase in temperature and/or pressure.

5. A minute portion of matter.

City Structures

Across

1. It is a small simple house.

3. It is a huge, fancy building where a king or queen lives.

4. You can put your money for safe keeping.

5. It is a curved structure that you will see when you enter the city.

Down

2. It is a city structure built by people.

3. Some people worship in here.

Matter

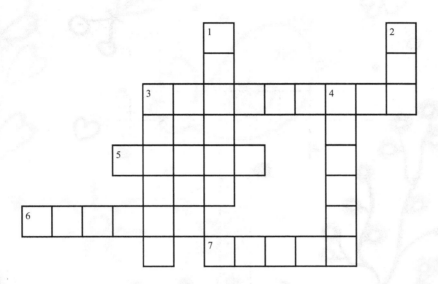

Across

3. Two or more atoms joined together.

5. The basic units of matter.

6. Property of matter that state the quality of shining by reflecting light.

7. Matter that has a definite shape and volume.

Down

1. It measures the amount of space that a substance or an object takes up .

2. Matter that does not have a definite shape or volume.

3. It is a substance that has inertia and occupies physical space.

4. Matter that does not have a shape but has volume.

Farm

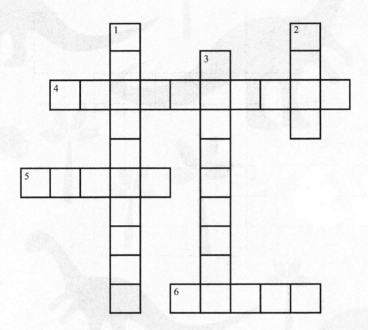

Across

4. It is the application of controlled amounts of water to plants at needed intervals.

5. An area of open land, especially one planted with crops or pasture.

6. These are living plants grown by farmers.

Down

1. A chemical or natural substance added to soil or land to increase its fertility.

2. Increase by natural development, as any living organism

3. A versatile machine designed to efficiently harvest a variety of grain crops.

Tools

Across

3. It helps you find your way in the dark.

4. It is used to hold up an item of clothing in a closet.

5. A brace, band, or clasp used for strengthening or holding things together.

Down

1. It is a machine that makes a breeze.

2. is a tool with a characteristically shaped cutting edge of blade on its end.

3. It keeps things icy.

Body

Across

4. It has taste buds and helps us eat, taste and talk.

6. It is an irregular bone with a complex structure composed of bone and some hyaline cartilage.

8. it is the middle of the body, between the chest and the hips.

Down

1. It is the widest finger and next to the pointing finger.

2. It is also called the backbone.

3. It is a muscular organ located on the left side of the upper abdomen.

5. It grows at the end of your toes.

7. We use these to chew foods.

Time

Across

3. There are 60 _____ in an hour.

6. It is the twelfth month of the year.

7. The sun is up during the _____.

Down

1. There are 24 _____ in a day.

2. It is the second month of the year.

4. It is the part of the day and the early part of the night.

5. There are 60 _____ in a minute.

House

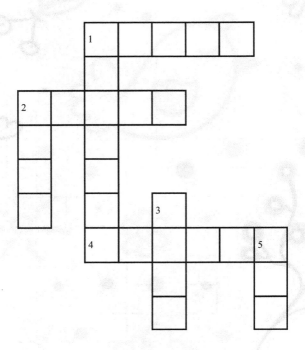

Across

1. A long, flat board fixed horizontally, usually against a wall or inside a cupboard so that objects can be stored on it.

2. A seat without a back or arms, typically resting on three or four legs or on a single pedestal.

4. It is a place in which a person bathes under a spray.

Down

1. These absorb a lot of liquid, and used for washing and cleaning.

2. We can wash our hands at a _____.

3. A large, soft piece of furniture that many people can sit on.

5. It is a piece of thick material that you put on a floor.

Weather

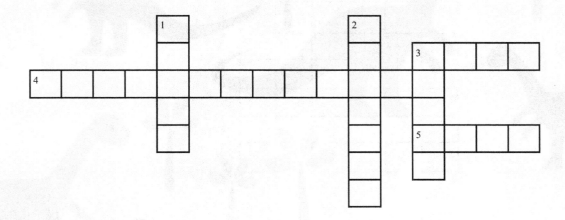

Across

3. It is an atmospheric water vapor frozen into ice crystals and falling in light white flakes or lying on the ground as a white layer.

4. A weather forecaster.

5. It is a water falling in drops condensed from vapor in the atmosphere.

Down

1. A visible mass of condensed water vapor floating in the atmosphere, typically high above the ground.

2. It is an arch of colors formed in the sky in certain circumstances.

3. A violent disturbance of the atmosphere with strong winds and usually rain, thunder, lightning, or snow.

Money

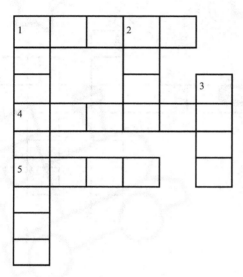

Across

1. A printed form, used instead of money, to make payments from your bank account.

4. Something that you will receive when you pay an amount that is higher than the bill.

5. It is a written statement of money that you owe for goods or services.

Down

1. A book containing blank checks or orders on a bank.

2. A flat, typically round piece of metal with an official stamp, used as money.

3. A very small unit of money and another word for penny.

Land and Water

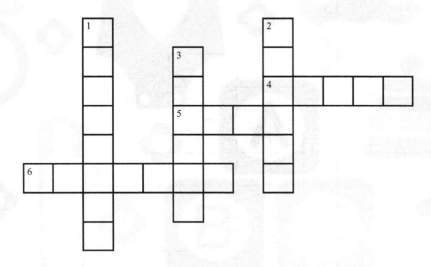

Across

4. It is a long, flowing natural stream of water.

5. A large body of water surrounded by land.

6. These are landforms alongside a body of water which consist of loose particles.

Down

1. It is a large landform that rises above the surrounding land in a limited area, usually in the form of a peak.

2. A large area covered chiefly with trees and undergrowth.

3. It is a low area between hills or mountains typically with a river running through it.

Science

Across

2. It is the basic unit of a chemical element.

5. Compound or substances that have been purified or prepared, especially artificially.

6. The remains of a prehistoric organism preserved in petrified form or as a mold or cast in rock.

Down

1. It refers to day-to-day temperature and precipitation activity.

3. It is an individual living thing, such as a plant, animal, bacterium, protest, or fungus.

4. It is the study of living organisms, divided into many specialized fields that cover their morphology, physiology, anatomy, behavior, origin, and distribution.

Autumn

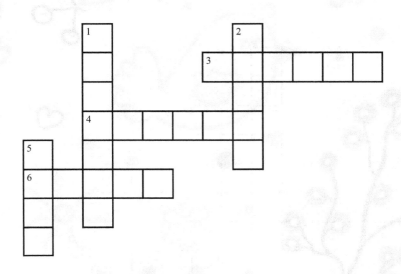

Across

3. The autumn _____ carries fine drops, each one a promise of the rain to come.

4. _____ of so many trees change colour in autumn.

6. Autumn is well known for its wet and _____ weather.

Down

1. Leaves are _____ during winter.

2. It means briskly cold winter weather.

5. A small shoot or branch usually without its leaves.

Body

Across

2. It is a limb that extends from the shoulder of the body.

3. Human _____ is the scientific study of the body's structures.

5. These are the sides of the face between the mouth area and the ear.

6. Soft, movable, and serve as the opening for food intake and in the articulation of sound and speech.

Down

1. It is the command center for the human nervous system.

4. It is the joint between your foot and leg.

Occupation

Across

2. A person whose occupation is mainly to cut, dress, groom, style and shave men's and boys' hair.

4. A person whose job is making and repairing wooden objects and structures.

5. A person who controls the flight of an aircraft.

6. One who is trained and licensed to heal the sick or injured.

Down

1. A person who provides and monitors patient care.

3. Qualified person who is trained in bookkeeping and in preparation, auditing and analysis of account

Musical Instrument

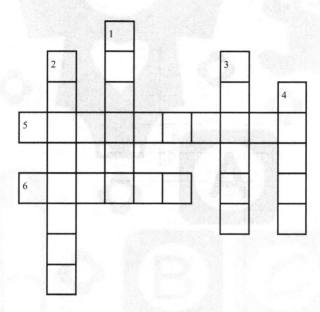

Across

5. is a musical instrument in the percussion family consisting of a frame, often of wood or plastic, with pairs of small metal jingles, called "zills".

6. It is sometimes known as a fiddle, is a wooden string instrument.

Down

1. Percussion instrument consisting of a circular flat or concave metal plate that is struck with a drumstick or is used in pairs struck glancing together.

2. It has a single-reed mouthpiece, a straight, cylindrical tube with an almost cylindrical bore, and a flared bell.

3. It is a fretted musical instrument that usually has six strings.

4. A wooden musical instrument with four strings, that is held vertically between the legs and is played by moving a bow across the strings.

Nutrients

Across

2. The sugar in milk.

4. are the sugars, starches and fibers found in fruits, grains, vegetables and milk products.

6. The body's use of energy from foods.

Down

1. There are no "bad" foods. All foods can be eaten in _____.

3. Beans are a non-meat (or vegetarian) source of this.

5. Also called as table sugar, organic compound, colourless sweet-tasting crystals that dissolve in water.

People

Across

3. A _____ is a person who is learning

4. A person who fights for a country.

6. A _____ is a group of people that work together towards a goal.

Down

1. A person who helps you learn.

2. _____ were Japanese warriors.

5. _____ scubas swim under the water and carry their own air in a tank on their back.

Weather

Across

3. It is the component of the Earth that is composed of all liquid water found on the planet.

4. _____ is a flash of light in the sky caused by an electrical storm.

Down

1. It is also known as sundown, is the daily disappearance of the Sun below the horizon due to Earth's rotation.

2. It is a type of large storm system having a circular or spiral system of violent winds, typically hundreds of kilometers or miles in diameter.

3. A _____ is a strong storm with high winds and rain.

5. It is traditionally an atmospheric phenomenon in which dust, smoke, and other dry particulates obscure the clarity of the sky.

Adjective

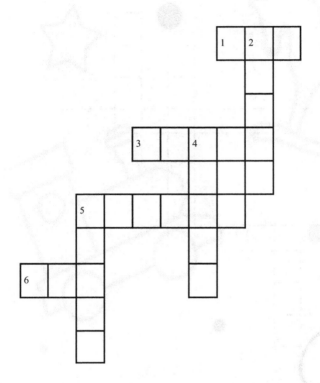

Across

1. The opposite of good.

3. It is the darkest color, the result of the absence or complete absorption of visible light.

5. When you are scared.

6. It is above average size.

Down

2. It means rouse from sleep.

4. When things look the same.

5. When you are very mad.

Music

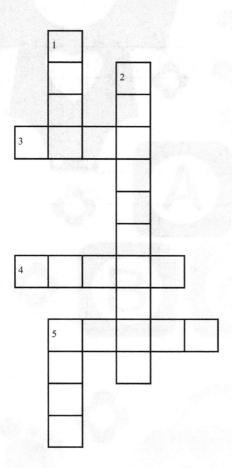

Across

3. A main accent or rhythmic unit in music or poetry.

4. It means to indicate raising the volume of the music.

5. It is any harmonic set of pitches consisting of multiple notes.

Down

1. It is the pitch and duration of a sound, and also its representation in musical notation.

2. Accuracy of pitch in singing, or on a stringed instrument such as a guitar.

5. It is a musical symbol used to indicate the pitch of written notes.

House

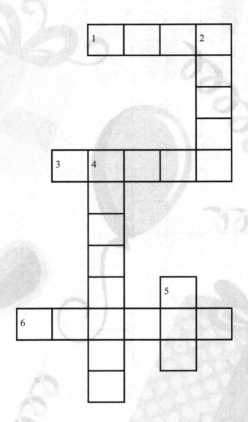

Across

1. It can be an upper storey or attic in a building, directly under the roof or just a storage space under the roof usually accessed by a ladder.

3. You can cook food on a _____.

6. _____ cleaner is a device used to clean rugs and floors.

Down

2. It is a piece of furniture with a flat top and legs.

4. A _____ holds garbage.

5. A small, simple, single-storey house or shelter.

Christmas

Across

3. Christmas present is a _____ given in celebration of Christmas.

4. A song of praise or joy, especially for Christmas.

6. It is often rung to signal the start of this service.

Down

1. _____ Claus is an imaginary fat man with a white beard and a red suit who gives toys to children at Christmas.

2. Gift-_____ is a symbol of love. During Christmas, it should remind us of the gift of Christ that we were given 2000 years ago and are continually given each and every day.

5. Literally means "messenger," and it is prominent role that it takes part in the Christmas story.

Farm

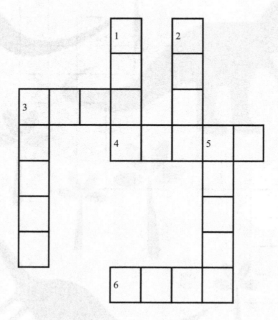

Across

3. It is a male cow.

4. It is a type of barrier.

6. It is a bird that has a webbed feet and a flattened bill.

Down

1. It is a young cow.

2. A usually large building for the storage of farm products or feed and usually for the housing of farm animals or equipment.

3. It is a young rabbit.

5. It is a baby chicken.

School

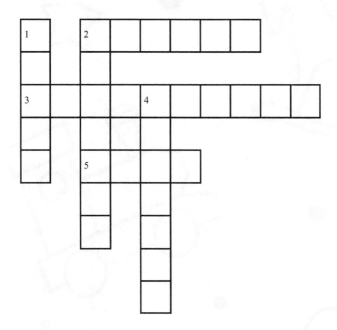

Across

2. It is an object that you write or draw with.

3. is a measuring instrument, typically made of transparent plastic or glass, for measuring angles.

5. It is a formal test that you take to show your knowledge or ability in a particular subject, or to obtain a qualification.

Down

1. A piece or sheet of paper with something written.

2. A task or problem in school that requires careful work over a long period of time.

4. _____ comprehension is the ability to process text and understand its meaning.

Occupation

Across

3. A person whose occupation is making fitted clothes such as suits, pants, and jackets to fit individual customers.

4. Someone who captures fish and other animals from a body of water, or gathers shellfish.

6. The creator or originator of any written work such as a book or play, and is also considered a writer.

Down

1. Someone who diagnoses and treats problems with a patient's teeth, gums, and related parts of the mouth.

2. Experts in medicines and their use.

5. A person who creates poetry.

Mathematics

Across

3. The process of uniting two or more numbers into one sum, represented by the symbol +.

4. It is a mathematical operation that tells us the difference between two numbers.

6. _____ number is an integer which is "evenly divisible" by two.

Down

1. The basic idea of _____ is repeated addition.

2. It is the answer in Multiplication.

5. _____ number is an integer which is not a multiple of two.

Astronomy

Across

2. They are tiny planets that mostly orbit between Mars and Jupiter.

3. It is the gas that surrounds a planet.

5. It is the science that studies the universe.

Down

1. A person who studies Astronomy and learn about objects in the universe.

2. They goes up into space to explore.

4. Everything is made up of _____.

5. These are beautiful light in the near-polar sky.

School

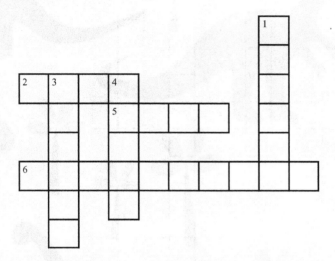

Across

2. To make a picture of something or someone with a pencil or pen.

5. To look at words or symbols and understand what they mean.

6. It is a collection of words and their definitions.

Down

1. A spoken or written reply or response to a question.

3. To say a piece of writing aloud from memory, or to publicly say a list of things.

4. To make marks that represent letters, words, or numbers on a surface, such as paper.

Family

Across

5. The mother of one's father or mother.

6. A child of a person's aunt or uncle.

Down

1. The brother of one's father or mother or the husband of one's aunt.

2. A woman on her wedding day or just before and after the event.

3. The relationship between brothers.

4. A man who is about to get married.

People

Across

4. A violent destructive whirling wind accompanied by a funnel-shaped cloud that progresses in a narrow path over the land.

5. A natural movement of air of any velocity.

6. The warmest season of the year.

Down

1. A tornado or a whirlwind

2. It is the light and heat that comes from the sun

3. An overflow of water that submerges land that is usually dry.

Sports

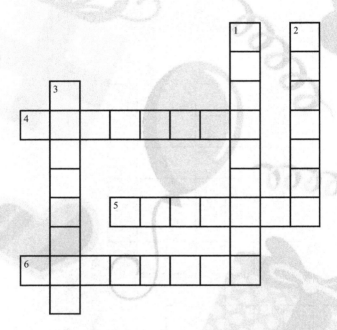

Across

4. It is a team sport played with a spherical ball between two teams of eleven players, and also commonly known as soccer.

5. It is a target sport and recreational activity in which a player rolls or throws a bowling ball toward pins or another target.

6. A set of international sports competitions that happen once every four years.

Down

1. It is a collection of sporting events that involve competitive running, jumping, throwing, and walking.

2. It is a group of three related combat sports.

3. A game similar to baseball but played with a larger, softer ball.

Astronomy

Across

5. It is a group of stars that forms an imaginary outline or pattern on the celestial sphere.

6. is the third planet from the Sun and the only astronomical object known to harbor life.

Down

1. It happens when the moon blocks out light from the sun or the earth's shadow goes across the moon.

2. _____ moon is smaller than a half moon.

3. Is is an enormous group of stars.

4. It is a small, icy object that orbits the sun.

Shapes

Across
2. It is a quadrilateral with four right angles.

4. A _____ is a curve that winds in on itself like the shape of snail shells.

5. A _____ has four, equally long sides which are at right angles to each other.

Down
1. A _____ is a four-sided figure with two parallel sides.

3. It has three sides.

5. A _____ is a ball-shaped object.

Matter

Across

4. When a solid is changing to a liquid form.

5. It is a combination of two or more substances that are not chemically united and do not exist in fixed proportions to each other.

6. _____ change is when matter changes how it looks but not what it is made of.

Down

1. _____ change is when matter changes and creates a new matter.

2. When a liquid is changing to a solid form.

3. The size, shape, luster, color and the texture of an object.

5. It is a measure of the amount of matter in an object.

Weather

Across

2. _____ cloud is a thin wispy fibrous cloud at high altitudes , composed of ice particles.

4. A wind blowing from directly in front, opposing forward motion.

5. is the amount of water vapor present in air.

6. It diffused matter such as smoke or fog, suspended floating in the air and impairing its transparency.

Down

1. It is situated or moving in the opposite direction to that in which the wind is blowing.

3. A single drop of rain.

Time

Across
4. A period of one hundred years.
5. The middle period of the night.
6. A special anniversary of an event, especially one celebrating twenty-five or fifty years of a reign or activity.

Down
1. A time in the future or after the time you have mentioned.
2. The time from noon or lunchtime.
3. The usual time when someone goes to bed.

Body

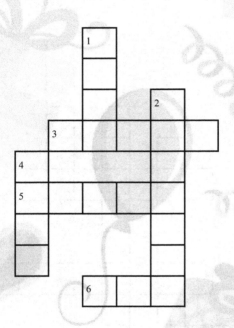

Across

3. The joint where your arm bends.

5. The joint where the foot joins the leg.

6. Either one of the two long body parts that join the top of your body at the shoulder and that end at the hand or wrist.

Down

1. The back part of your foot that is below the ankle.

2. The part of the arm between the elbow and the wrist.

4. The front part of the head that has the eyes, nose, and mouth on it.

School

Across

2. When you _____, you find out something new.

5. A formal test of a person's knowledge or proficiency in a particular subject.

6. A set of pupils taught together.

Down

1. A school for developing the minds of children.

3. Perform a scientific procedure, especially in a laboratory, to determine something.

4. A teacher who prepares pupils for examination.

Tools

Across

2. An instrument used for cutting cloth, paper, and other thin material.

5. It is a tool that is used for turning screws.

Down

1. A tool with two handles at one end and two hard, flat, metal parts at the other.

3. A _____ is a device that opens can.

4. A tool with a heavy metal head mounted at right angles at the end of a handle, used for jobs such as breaking things and driving in nails.

6. A hand tool, power tool, or machine with a rotating cutting tip used for making holes.

Shapes

Across

3. A plane figure with five straight sides and five angles.

4. It looks like a diamond.

6. Having a rounded and slightly elongated outline or shape like that of an egg.

Down

1. A solid object with a square base and four triangular sides that form a point at the top.

2. A half of a circle or of its circumference.

5. A plane figure with eight straight sides and eight angles.

Body

Across

2. The front surface of a person's body between the neck and the abdomen.

4. A band or bundle of fibrous tissue in a human.

6. Any of the fine threadlike strands growing from the skin of human.

Down

1. One of the hard parts of the skeleton of a vertebrate.

3. The upper joint of the human arm and the part of the body between this and the neck.

5. The thin layer of tissue forming the natural outer covering of the body of a person.

Tools

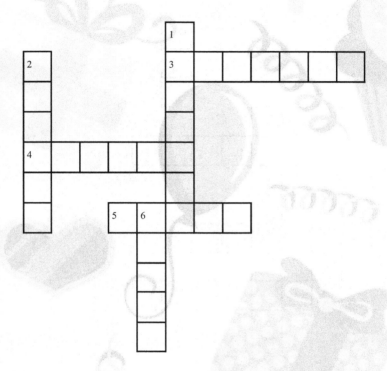

Across

3. It is also called toolkit, tool chest or work box.

4. is a tool with a long handle that is used for lifting.

5. is a metal object similar to a nail, with a raised spiral line around it.

Down

1. A device for fastening together sheets of paper with a staple or staples.

2. It is a sharp power tool that's used for cutting curvy lines in wood or other materials.

6. A device made of wood or metal that is used to hold two things together tightly.

Family

Across

3. A man in relation to his child or children.

5. A woman in relation to her child or children.

6. A son of one's brother or sister, or of one's brother-in-law or sister-in-law.

Down

1. A daughter of one's brother or sister, or of one's brother-in-law or sister-in-law.

2. A girl or woman in relation to her parents.

4. One's male child.

Astronomy

Across

3. The angular distance of a celestial body from the horizon measured along the vertical circle passing through the body.

5. is the sixth planet from the Sun and the second-largest in the Solar System, after Jupiter.

Down

1. is the fifth planet from the Sun and the largest in the Solar System.

2. It is the second planet from the Sun

3. The entire atmosphere surrounding the earth.

4. It is the seventh planet from the Sun.

Parts of a Tree

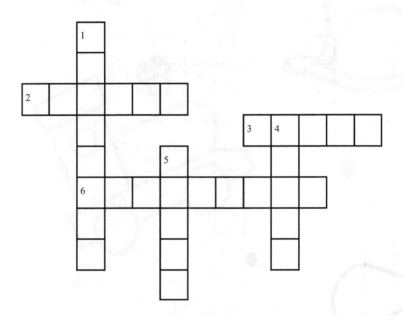

Across

2. These are the part of the crown of a tree and these convert energy into food.

3. It is made up of the leaves and branches at the top of a tree.

6. It is dead sapwood in the center of the trunk.

Down

1. Provide the support to distribute the leaves efficiently for the type of tree and the environment.

4. Part of the tree that grows underground.

5. It provides its shape and support and holds up the crown.

Family

Across

2. These are two offspring produced by the same pregnancy.

3. A person, typically one more remote than a grandparent, from whom one is descended.

6. A man in relation to his child or children.

Down

1. Each of two or more children or offspring having one or both parents in common; a brother or sister.

4. A woman or girl in relation to other daughters and sons of her parents.

5. Group of families, who originally came from the same family.

School

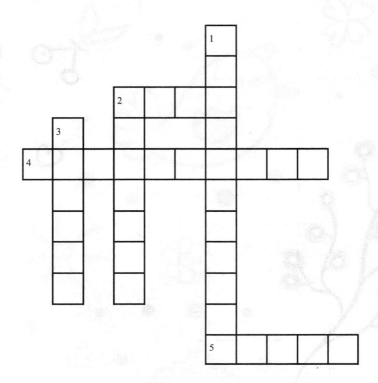

Across

2. A _____ determines if you have learned something or not and it is also called examination.

4. A person's _____ is the group of words that person understand.

5. It means instruct, educate, train, to provide knowledge or skill.

Down

1. Able to learn and understand things easily.

2. A _____ is someone who helps you learn.

3. The letters A, E, I, O and U.

House

Across

3. It is a room in the home or hotel for personal hygiene activities, generally containing a toilet, a bathtub, a shower, or both.

4. The covering that forms the top of a house.

5. It is a room or part of a room used for cooking and food preparation in a dwelling or in a commercial establishment.

Down

1. A building where a car is kept, built next to or as part of a house.

2. It is a panel that covers an opening in a building, room or vehicle.

3. The part of a building or house that is wholly or partly below ground level.

Tools

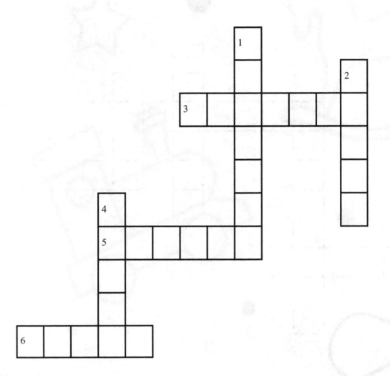

Across

3. It is one of power tools or machine tools used for grinding, and a type of machine using an abrasive wheel as the cutting tool.

5. It is a vertical or inclined set of rungs or steps.

6. Sometimes called line gauge, a device used to measure or draw straight lines.

Down

1. A hand tool with two cutting blades for clipping fingernails, hedges, etc.

2. An object with short pieces of stiff hair, plastic, or wire attached to a base or handle, used for cleaning, arranging your hair, or painting.

4. It is a garment covering the whole hand.

Animals

Across

2. It is a large animal that leaps or springs on its big, strong back legs and uses its heavy tail for balance.

5. is a large crocodile with an armored body, short legs, a muscular tail and a long, rounded snout.

6. A farm animal with thick wool that eats grass and is kept for its wool, skin, and meat.

Down

1. A large reptile with a hard skin that lives in and near rivers and lakes in hot, wet parts of the world.

3. These are mammals with long legs, a big-lipped snout and a humped back.

4. A sea mammal that is large, smooth, and grey, with a long, pointed mouth.

Animals

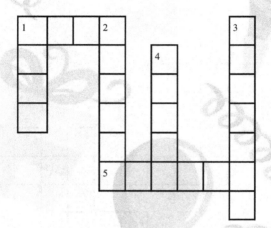

Across

1. It is a four-legged, hoofed animal with antlers.

5. An animal which lives in or near water and has a thick shell covering its body into which it can move its head and legs for protection.

Down

1. A waterbird with a broad blunt bill, short legs, webbed feet, and a waddling gait.

2. A small animal with long ears and large front teeth that moves by jumping on its long back legs, or the meat of this animal eaten as food.

3. A small animal covered in fur with a short tail and large spaces in each side of its mouth for storing food.

4. A large, wild cat that has a coat of usually yellow or orange fur and black stripes and that lives in Asia.

Feelings and Emotions

Across

3. It is a feeling of joy, pleasure, or good fortune .

5. Feeling or showing sorrow or unhappy.

6. A situation in which people are uncertain about what to do or are unable to understand something clearly.

Down

1. A feeling of great pleasure and happiness.

2. The state or condition of being free from disturbance or violent activity.

4. It is the willingness to tolerate a difficult or unpleasant situation.

Desserts and Sweets

Across

3. It is a sweet food made by baking a mixture of flour, eggs, sugar, and fat in an oven.

4. It is a usually sweet, brown food preparation of roasted and ground cacao seeds.

5. A soft candy made from sugar, butter, and milk or cream.

Down

1. A light cookie made with egg white, sugar, and usually ground almonds or coconut.

2. It is a clear tasteless powder that is used to make liquids become firm, for example when you are making desserts.

4. A dessert or sweet sauce made with milk, eggs, and sugar.

Animals

Across

1. A small creature with smooth skin, big eyes, and long back legs which it uses for jumping.

3. An animal that lives in water, is covered with scales, and breathes by taking water in through its mouth.

4. A large bird of prey with a massive hooked bill and long broad wings, renowned for its keen sight and powerful soaring flight.

Down

1. A wild mammal belonging to the dog family that has a pointed face and ears, a wide tail covered in fur, and often reddish-brown fur.

2. It is a large African animal with a very long neck, long legs, and dark patches on its body.

5. It is a farm animal or a wild animal that is about the size of a sheep that usually has horns and a beard.

House

Across
5. A room in a house in which meals are eaten.
6. The lower surface of a room, on which one may walk.

Down
1. A room or area where food is prepared and cooked.
2. Room in a house or apartment that is used for relaxing in and entertaining guests.
3. A series of steps or flights of steps for passing from one level to another.
4. A room for sleeping.

Body

Across

1. We have ten toes on our _____.

4. These are dense patches of hair above the eyes.

6. These are flaps of skin that cover and protect our eyes.

7. Part of the face below the mouth.

Down

2. It is the joint in the middle of your arm.

3. It is our sense of hearing.

4. It give us a sense of sight.

5. These are long hairs on the edges of the eyelids.

Landforms

Across

2. A small cave with interesting or attractively shaped rocks.

3. A naturally raised area of land, not high as a mountain.

5. A large valley with very steep sides and usually a river flowing along the bottom.

Down

1. The narrow strip of land that borders the sea along a continent or an island.

2. A small valley or ravine originally worn away by running water and serving as a drainage after prolonged heavy rains.

4. A piece of land surrounded by water.

Sports

Across

2. A large, flat area surrounded by seats used for sports or entertainment.

3. Physical exercises and activities performed inside, often using equipment, especially when done as a subject at school.

5. It is the use of bicycles for transport, recreation, exercise or sport.

6. An activity requiring physical effort, carried out to sustain or improve health and fitness.

Down

1. A contest for the position of champion in a sport, often involving a series of games or matches.

4. The condition of being physically fit and healthy.

House

Across

2. It is a piece of furniture or a support used to elevate the foot.

3. A container, typically plastic or metal, for household refuse.

5. A container, operated by electricity, that stores food at a very cold temperature.

Down

1. It is a type of barrier enclosing or bordering a house.

2. Tables, chairs, beds and sofas are _____ inside the house.

4. It is a piece of land next to a house, with flowers, vegetables and other plants.

Shapes

Across

4. A flat shape with 4 straight sides that has a pair of opposite sides parallel.

5. A plane figure with four equal straight sides and four right angles.

6. A plane figure with nine straight sides and nine angles.

Down

1. A quadrilateral with two pairs of parallel sides.

2. It is a quadrilateral whose four sides can be grouped into two pairs of equal-length sides that are adjacent to each other.

3. It is a seven-sided polygon

Birthday

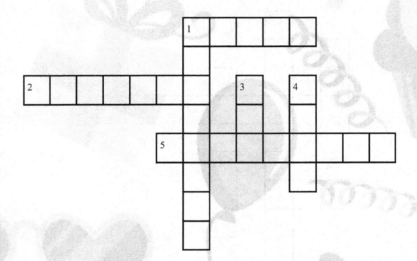

Across

1. An entertainer who wears funny clothes, has a painted face, and makes people laugh by performing tricks and behaving in a silly way.

2. A small, very thin rubber bag that you blow air into or fill with a light gas until it is round in shape, used for decoration at parties.

5. To take part in special enjoyable activities in order to show that a particular occasion is important like birthday.

Down

1. Small pieces of colored paper thrown during a celebration such as birthday.

3. The period of time someone has been alive.

4. Existing as a result of birth.

Nutrients

Across

4. Primary transporter of nutrients throughout the body and is necessary for all bodily functions.

5. Act or process in which living organisms utilize food substances.

6. A highly concentrated source of energy in the body.

Down

1. Includes sugars and starches.

2. This is produced in mammary glands of lactating animals.

3. A unit of heat used to measure the energy value of food.

Time

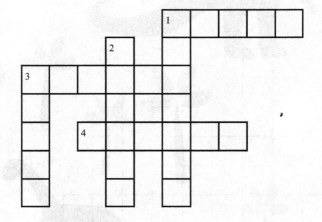

Across

1. If you want to know what time it is, look at a _____.

3. It is the season between summer and winter.

4. It is the eight month of the year.

Down

1. A _____ is 100 years.

2. The event that will happen after the present time.

3. It is the fourth month of the year.

Animals

Across

2. A wild animal of the cat family, with yellowish-brown fur and black spots, that can run faster than any other animal.

4. A soft sea creature with eight long arms called tentacles which it uses to catch food.

6. An animal that lives in the sea and has a long body covered with a hard shell, two large claws, and eight legs, or its flesh when used as food.

Down

1. It is a wild horse which has black and white stripes.

3. It is an even-toed hoofed mammal, but scientists think it is more closely related to whales and dolphins than other even-toed hoofed mammals.

5. A small creature with eight thin legs that catches insects in a web.

Transportation

Across

1. A large motor vehicle carrying passengers by road, typically one serving the public on a fixed route and for a fare.

2. A road vehicle with an engine, four wheels, and seats for a small number of people.

4. vehicle specially equipped for taking sick or injured people to and from the hospital, especially in emergencies.

Down

1. A vehicle composed of two wheels held in a frame one behind the other, propelled by pedals and steered with handlebars attached to the front wheel.

3. A medium-sized motor vehicle with a boxy shape and high roof, used for transporting goods or passengers.

5. A small vessel propelled on water by sails or an engine.

Transportation

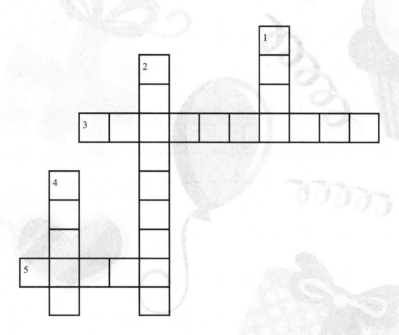

Across

3. A type of aircraft without wings, that has one or two sets of large blades that go round very fast on top.

5. A large, tall machine used for moving heavy objects by suspending them from a projecting arm or beam.

Down

1. A small, rugged automotive vehicle with a -ton capacity and a four-wheel drive.

2. A powerful tractor with a broad upright blade at the front for clearing ground.

4. A boat or ship for conveying passengers and goods, especially over a relatively short distance and as a regular service.

Astronomy

Across

2. It is used to describe things relating to the sun.

3. A vehicle used for space travel.

5. A distinctive pattern of stars used informally to organize a part of the sky.

6. It is a "dirty snowball" of ice and rocky debris, typically a few miles across, that orbits the Sun.

Down

1. An occasion when the sun disappears from view, either completely or partly, while the moon is moving between it and the earth.

4. A celestial body orbiting the earth or another planet.

People

Across

2. A _____ is the daughter of a king and queen.

3. An accredited diplomat sent by a country as its official representative to a foreign country.

5. A _____ is the son of a king and queen.

Down

1. A _____ is a hereditary ruler of a country.

2. A _____ is an elected leader of a country.

4. A _____ is the male ruler of an independent state.

Time

Across

2. A period of time by which something is late or postponed .

3. Coming or happening later than should have been the case.

5. Existing or occurring now.

6. The sun rises in the _____ .

Down

1. A period of ten years.

4. The period of time at the end of the day.

Occupation

Across

3. A person who is proficient in sports and other forms of physical exercise.

4. A person whose profession is acting on the stage, in movies, or on television.

5. A person who makes bread and cakes.

Down

1. A person who practices any of the various creative arts, such as a sculptor, novelist, poet, or film-maker.

2. A female ballet dancer.

4. An organized military force equipped for fighting on land.

Music

Across

5. A small flute sounding an octave higher than the ordinary one.

6. These are lengths of a flexible material that a musical instrument holds under tension so that they can vibrate freely, but controllably.

Down

1. In a quick and lively tempo.

2. A set of two or more kettle-drums played by one performer in an orchestra or band.

3. A musical instruments that you play by hitting them with your hand or an object such as a stick

4. The lowest female singing voice.

Adjectives

Across

3. Free from dirt, marks, or stains.

4. It is not open.

6. Not the same as another or each other.

Down

1. It is the color of the wood.

2. Color intermediate between green and violet, as of the sky or sea on a sunny day.

3. It has many colors.

5. The absence of light in a place.

Places

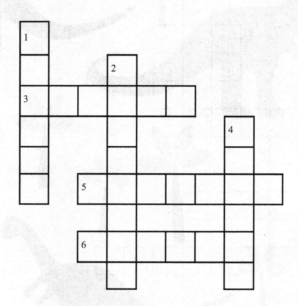

Across

3. It is a place where you learn things.

5. A place set apart to contain books, periodicals, and other material for reading.

6. A place where king and queen live.

Down

1. It exhibits arts, historic objects.

2. An institution providing medical and surgical treatment and nursing care for sick or injured people.

4. An area or arena in which commercial dealings are conducted.

Waterforms

Across

2. This is shallow and smaller than a stream.

5. It is a wide body of water found between islands.

6. It is a body of water surrounded by land.

Down

1. This is the smallest body of water.

3. This is the widest and largest body of water in the world.

4. is a place where water flows over the edge of a steep.

Places

Across

3. A place where you can buy bread and cakes .

5. A _____ store that sells objects such as rings and necklaces that people wear as decoration.

6. A building where Christians do religious activities.

Down

1. A _____ store where people can buy books.

2. A _____ store where people can buy medicines, beauty products, etc.

4. A place where planes take off and land, with buildings for passengers to wait for the planes.

Matter

Across

3. The smallest particle of a substance that has the same properties as the substance.

4. A tiny, charged particle in the nucleus of an atom.

5. One or two letters that represent the name of an element.

Down

1. The central part of an atom that holds the protons and neutrons.

2. A substance formed when atoms of two or more elements join together.

Plants

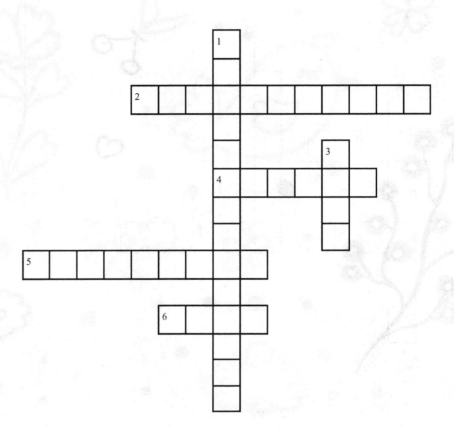

Across

2. The area where photosynthesis takes place that contains chlorophyll.

4. A shoot of a plant.

5. When a seed or spore begins to grow.

6. A plant that is not valued where it is growing and is usually of vigorous growth.

Down

1. The method in which green plants and other organisms use sunlight to process nourishment from water and carbon dioxide.

3. A round root of some plants from which the plant grows.

Verb

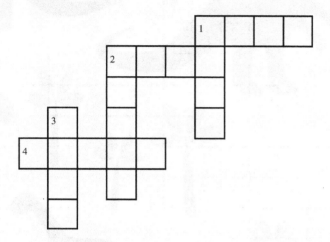

Across

1. Makes musical sounds with the voice, especially words with a set tune.

2. Bite and work (food) in the mouth with the teeth, especially to make it easier to swallow.

4. It moves rhythmically to music, typically following a set sequence of steps.

Down

1. To move through water by moving the body or parts of the body.

2. To take hold of something, especially something that is moving through the air.

3. To move along by putting one foot in front of the other, allowing each foot to touch the ground before lifting the next.

Christmas

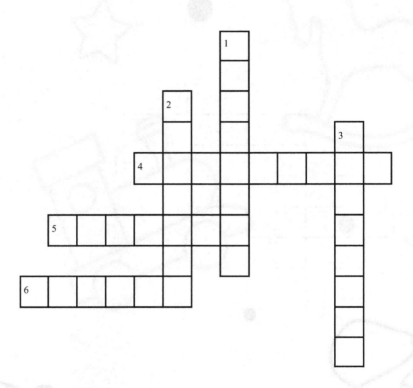

Across

4. The small town in the Middle East believed to be the birthplace of Jesus Christ.

5. The start of a year or the period just before and after 1 January.

6. The title of Jesus (also used as His name)

Down

1. A person who looks after sheep.

2. A thing given to somebody as a gift.

3. A deer with large antlers found in some cold climates (believed to pull the sleigh for Santa Claus or Father Christmas)

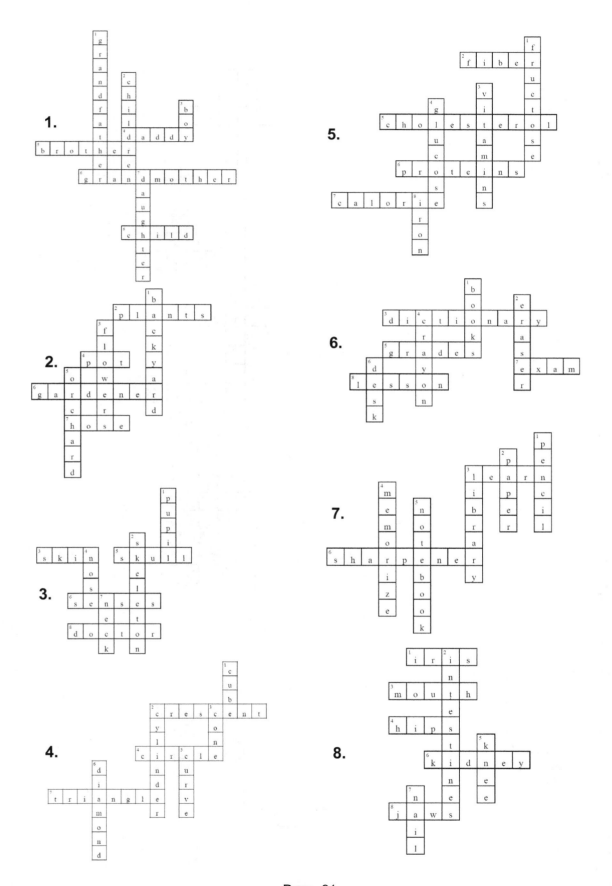

1.

Across:
4. daddy
5. brother
6. grandmother
8. child

Down:
1. grandfather
2. child
3. boy
7. daughter

2.

2. plants
4. pot
6. gardener
7. hose

Down:
1. backyard
3. flower
5. soccer
hard

3.

3. skin
5. skull
6. senses
8. doctor

Down:
1. pupil
2. skeleton
4. nose

4.

2. crescent
4. circle
7. triangle

Down:
1. cube
3. cone
5. curve
6. diamond
cylinder

5.

2. fiber
5. cholesterol
6. proteins
7. calorie

Down:
1. fructose
3. vitamins
4. glucose
8. iron

6.

3. dictionary
5. grades
7. exam
8. lesson

Down:
1. book
2. eraser
4. notebook
desk

7.

3. learn
6. sharpener

Down:
1. pencil
2. paper
3. library
4. memorize
5. notebook

8.

1. iris
3. mouth
4. hips
6. kidney
8. jaws

Down:
2. intestine
5. knee
7. nail

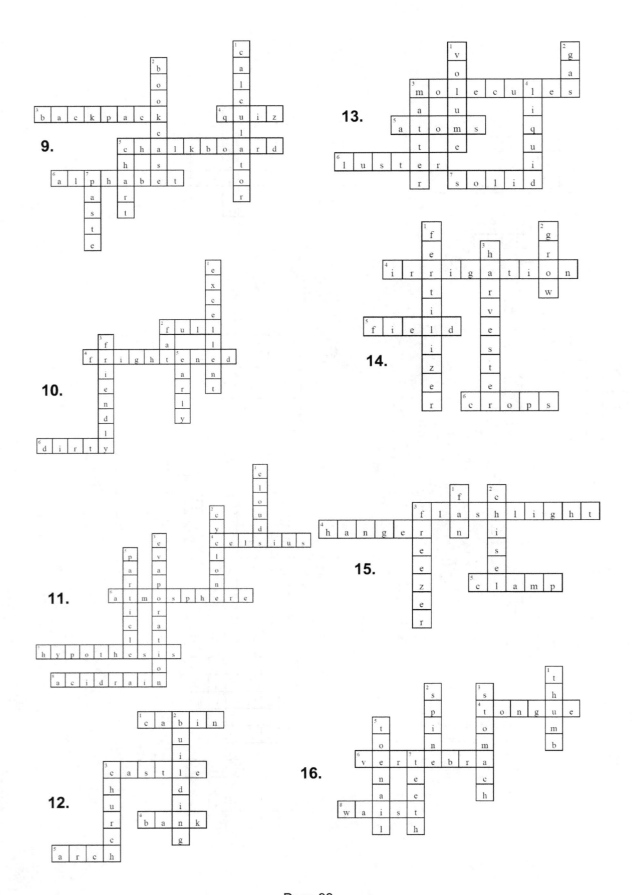

9.

10.

11.

12.

13.

14.

15.

16.

17.

Down: hour
Across: minutes, december, day
Down: february, evening, seconds

18. shelf, stool, sink, sponge, shower, sofa, rug

19. cloud, meteorologist, rainbow, snow, storm, rain

20. check, choice, cent, change, checkbook, bill

21. mountain, beaches, valley, lake, river, forest

22. weather, atom, organism, chemicals, fossils, foggy, bront

23. fall, breeze, leaves, twig, windy, crisp

24. brain, arm, anatomy, cheek, lips

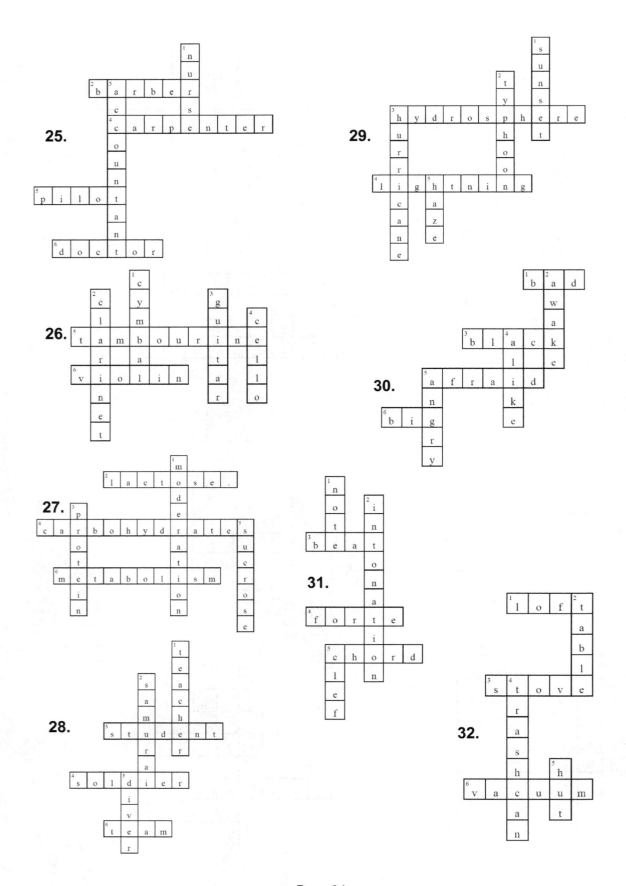

25.

26.

27.

28.

29.

30.

31.

32.

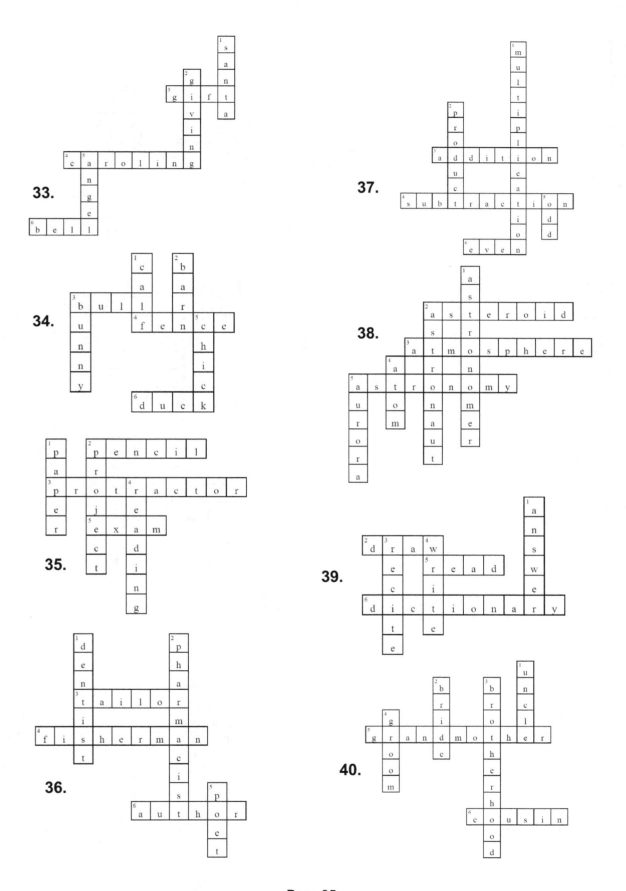

33.

34.

35.

36.

37.

38.

39.

40.

41.

42.

43.

44.

45.

46.

47.

48.

49.

50.

51.

52.

53.

54.

55.

56.

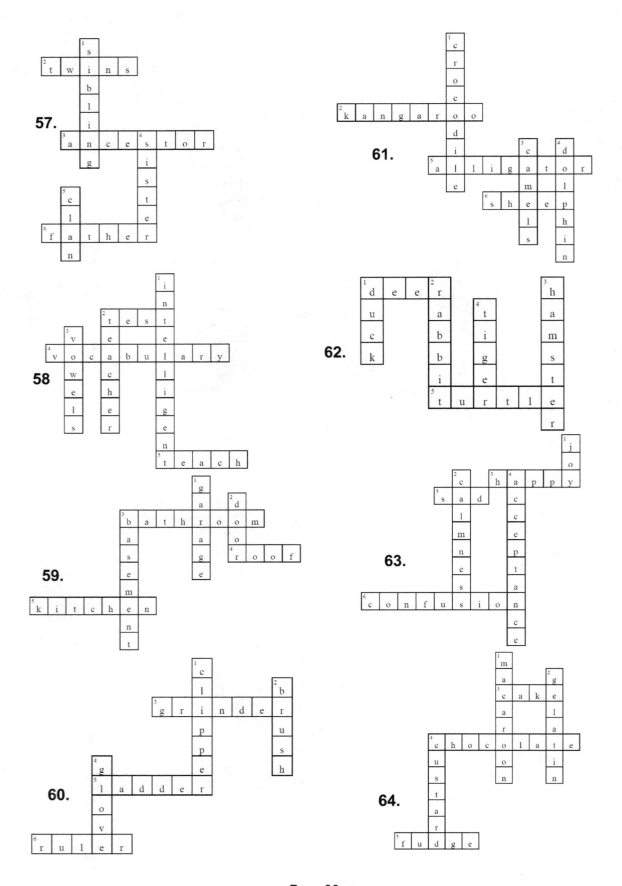

57.

Down: s, b, l, i, g (sibling)
2. twins
3. ancestor
5. clan
6. father

61.

Down: crocodile
2. kangaroo
5. alligator
6. sheep
camels, dolphin

58

1. in...
2. test
3. vowels
4. vocabulary
teacher
intelligent
5. teach

62.

1. deer / duck
2. rabbit
3. hamster
4. tiger
5. turtle

59.

1. garage
2. door
3. bathroom
4. roof
basement
5. kitchen

63.

1. joy
2. calmness
happy
3. acceptance
5. sad
6. confusion

60.

1. clippe...
2. brush
3. grinder
4. glove
5. ladder
6. ruler

64.

1. macaron
2. gelatin
3. cake
custard
4. chocolate
5. fudge

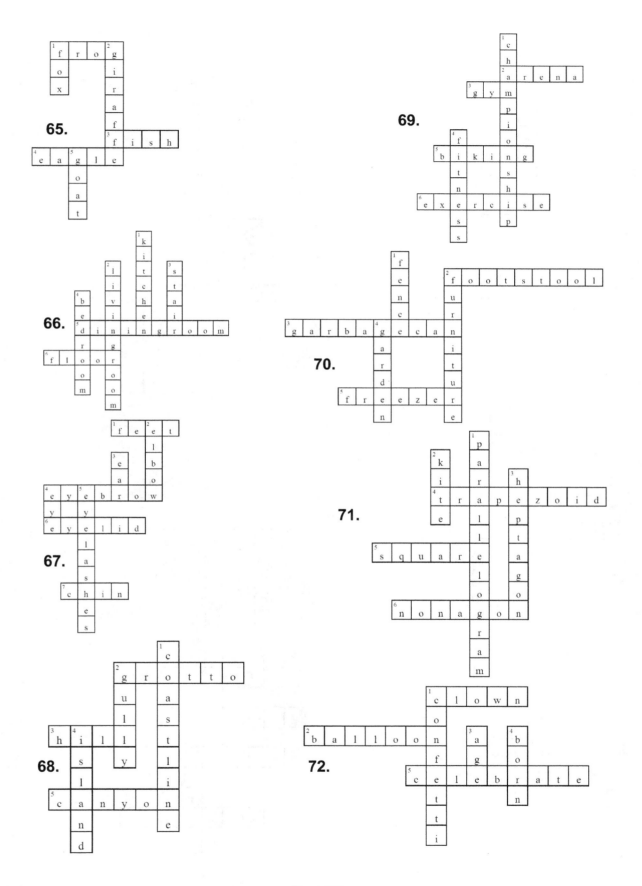

65.

66.

67.

68.

69.

70.

71.

72.

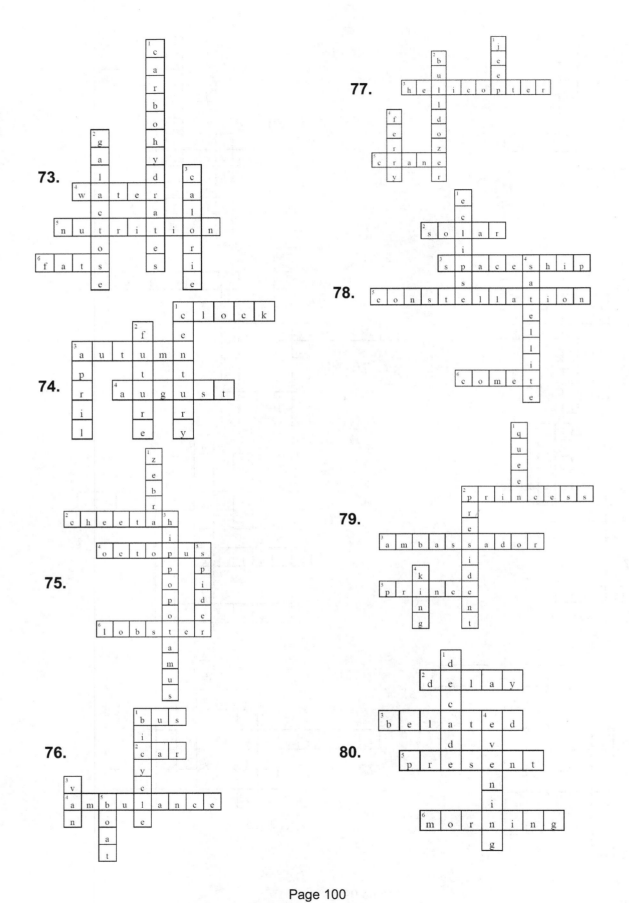

73.

74.

75.

76.

77.

78.

79.

80.

81.

82.

83.

84.

85.

86.

87.

88.

Across:
2. chloroplast
4. sprout
5. germinate
6. weed

Down:
1. photosynthesis
3. bulb

89.

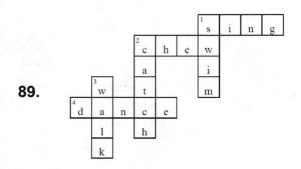

1. sing
2. chew
3. walk
4. dance
swim
eat
math

90.

Across:
4. bethlehem
5. new year
6. christ

Down:
1. shepherd
2. presents
3. reindeer

Conclusion

Thank you again for buying this book!   I hope you enjoyed with my book. Finally, if you like this book, please take the time to share your thoughts and post a review on Amazon. It'd be greatly appreciated! Thank you!

Next Steps
– Write me an honest review about the book –
I truly value your opinion and thoughts and I will incorporate them into my next book, which is already underway.

Get more free bonus here

www.funspace.club
Follow us : facebook.com/funspaceclub

Send email to get answer & solution here : funspaceclub18@gmail.com

Find us on Amazon

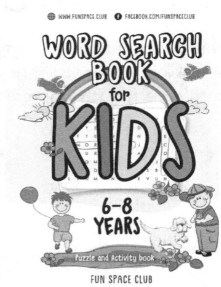

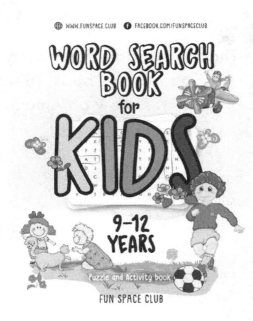

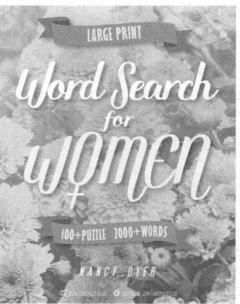

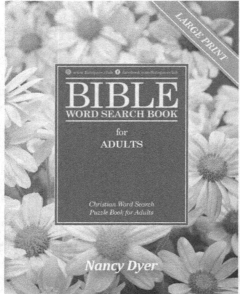

Find us on Amazon

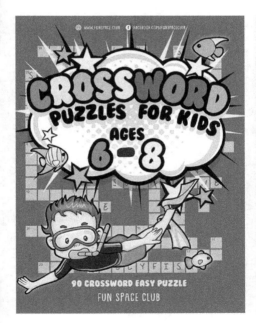

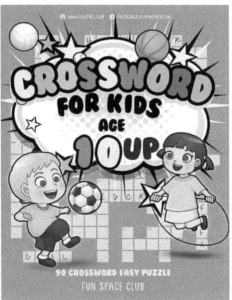

CPSIA information can be obtained
at www.ICGtesting.com
Printed in the USA
LVHW060149250821
696039LV00027BA/706